Mámáns,
they make the world go around.

Special mention for my mums:
Amy, Nouri, Noushin & Mojgán ján

"While they are at your side,
love these little ones to the uttermost.
Forget yourself.
Serve them;
care for them,
lavish all your tenderness on them.
Value your good fortune while it is with you,
and let nothing of the sweetness of their babyhood go unprized.
Fill up their days with happiness,
and share with them their mirth and innocent delights.
Childhood is but for a day.
Ere you are aware it will be gone with all its gifts forever."

George Townshend

The Persian Alphabet

We want to simplify your Persian learning journey as it is such a unique & enigmatic language. There are 32 official Persian letters. The letters change form depending on their position in a word or when they appear separate from other letters. For example, the letter g̲h̲ayn غ has four ways of being written depending on where it appears in any given word:

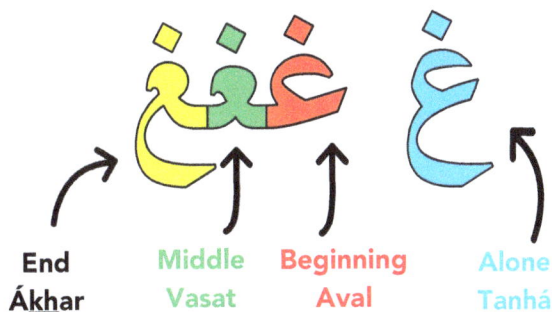

غـ ـغـ ـغـ غ

End	Middle	Beginning	Alone
Ák̲h̲ar	Vasat	Aval	Tanhá

It is important to note that Persian books are read from right to left (←).
There are 7 separate/stand-alone letters that do not connect in the same way to adjacent letters (these will be depicted in blue). They are:

Stand alone
Tanhá vámístan

و ژ ز ر ذ د ا

The short vowels a, e & o are usually omitted in literature and are depicted by markings above & below letters (ﹷ). They are not allocated a letter name, unlike their long vowel counterparts á: alef, í: ye & ú: váv (و ی آ).

Englisi	Farsi		Englisi	Farsi		Englisi	Farsi
A a	اَ أَ أَ		M m	م مـمـم mím		Y y	ى يـيـى ye
Á á	آ ا ا 'alef		N n	ن نـنـن nún		Z z	ذ ذذ zál
B b	ب بـبـب Be		O o	اُ أُ أُ		Z z	ز زز ze
D d	د دد dál		P p	پ پـپـپ pe		Z z	ض ضـضـض zád
E e	اِ ٍٍٍِ		Q q	ق قـقـق qáf		Z z	ظ ظـظـظ zá
F f	ف فـفـف fe		R r	ر رر re		Ch ch	چ چـچـچ che
G g	گ گـگـگ gáf		S s	س سـسـس sin		Gh gh	غ غـغـغ ghayn
H h	ه هـهـه he		S s	ص صـصـص sád		Kh kh	خ خـخـخ khe
H h	ح حـحـح he		S s	ث ثـثـث se		Sh sh	ش شـشـش shín
Í í	ى يـيـى ye		T t	ت تـتـت te		Zh zh	ژ ژژ zhe
J j	ج جـجـج jim		T t	ط طـطـط tá		'	ع عـعـع ayn
K k	ک کـکـک káf		Ú ú	و وو váv			
L l	ل لـلل lám		V v	و وو váv			

Letter Guide ©

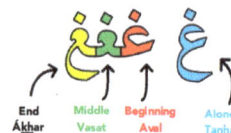

End
Ákhar

Middle
Vasat

Beginning
Aval

Alone
Tanhá

Pronunciation Guide©

Persian	English	Pronunciation
اَ	a	<u>a</u>nt
آ	á	<u>a</u>rm
ب	b	<u>b</u>at
د	d	<u>d</u>og
اِ	e	<u>e</u>nd
ف	f	<u>f</u>un
گ	g	<u>g</u>o
ه	h	<u>h</u>at
ح	h	<u>h</u>at
ی	í	m<u>ee</u>t
ج	j	<u>j</u>et
ک	k	<u>k</u>ey
ل	l	<u>l</u>ove
م	m	<u>m</u>e
ن	n	<u>n</u>ap
اُ	o	<u>o</u>n
پ	p	<u>p</u>at
ق	q/gh*	me<u>r</u>ci
ر	r	<u>r</u>un
س	s	<u>s</u>un
ص	s	<u>s</u>un
ث	s	<u>s</u>un

Persian	English	Pronunciation
ت	t	<u>t</u>op
ط	t	<u>t</u>op
و	ú	m<u>oo</u>n
و	v	<u>v</u>an
ی	y	<u>y</u>es
ذ	z	<u>z</u>oo
ز	z	<u>z</u>oo
ض	z	<u>z</u>oo
ظ	z	<u>z</u>oo
چ	<u>ch</u>	<u>ch</u>air
غ	<u>gh</u>*	me<u>r</u>ci
خ	<u>kh</u>*	ba<u>ch</u>
ش	<u>sh</u>	<u>sh</u>are
ژ	<u>zh</u>	plea<u>s</u>ure
ع	'	uh-<u>o</u>h†

*	: guttural sound from back of throat
†	: glottal stop, breathing pause
ّ	: Indicates a double letter
ً	: Indicates the letter n sound
لا	: Indicates combination of letter l & á (lá)
ای	: Indicates the long í sound (ee in m<u>ee</u>t)
ایِ	: Indicates the long í sound (ee in m<u>ee</u>t)
(...)	: Indicates colloquial use

happy

kho<u>sh</u>hál

خوشحال

á: as (a) in <u>a</u>rm

sad

ghamgín

غَمگین

í: as (ee) in m<u>ee</u>t

upset

náráhat

نَارَاحَت

á: as (a) in a̲rm

angry

kha<u>sh</u>mgín

خَشمگین

(a'sebání)

í: as (ee) in m<u>ee</u>t

á: as (a) in <u>a</u>rm

frustrated

hers khordan

حِرص خوردَن

hopeless

náomíd

نااُمید

á: as (a) in <u>a</u>rm

í: as (ee) in m<u>ee</u>t

curious

konjkáv

كُنجكاو

á: as (a) in <u>a</u>rm

tired

<u>kh</u>asteh

خَسِته

fearful/scared

tarsnák

تَرسناک

á: as (a) in a<u>r</u>m

surprised

mote'ajjeb

مُتِعَجِّب

(gháfel gír)

á: as (a) in arm
í: as (ee) in meet

confused

sardargom

سَردَرگُم

(gíj)

í: as (ee) in m<u>ee</u>t

bored

hoseleh sar rafteh

حوصِله سَر رَفته

calm

árám

آرام

á: as (a) in <u>a</u>rm

excited

hayeján zadeh

هَیِجان زَدِه

á: as (a) in a̲rm

empathetic

delsúzí

دِلسوزی

(hamdardí)

ú: as (oo) in m<u>oo</u>n
í: as (ee) in m<u>ee</u>t

anxious

delvápas

دِلوِاپَس

(del s͟húreh)

á: as (a) in <u>a</u>rm
ú: as (oo) in m<u>oo</u>n

proud

mofta<u>kh</u>ar

مُفتَخَر

very good

kheylí khúb
خِیلی خوب

í: as (ee) in m<u>ee</u>t
ú: as (oo) in m<u>oo</u>n

jealous

hasúd

حَسود

ú: as (oo) in m<u>oo</u>n

satisfied

rází

راضى

á: as (a) in <u>a</u>rm
í: as (ee) in m<u>ee</u>t

embarrassed

<u>sh</u>armandeh

شَرمَندِه

nervous

a'sabí

عَصَبى

í: as (ee) in m<u>ee</u>t

irritated

a'sáb kharáb

أَعصاب خَراب

á: as (a) in arm

grumpy

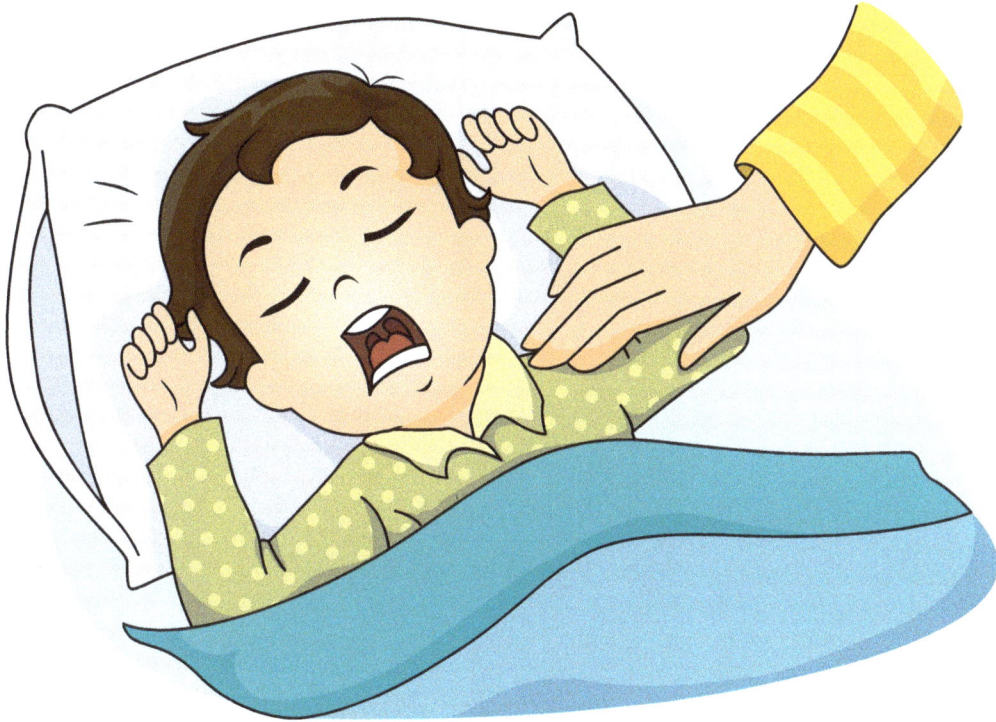

bad a<u>kh</u>lá<u>gh</u>

بَد اخلاق

á: as (a) in <u>ar</u>m

lonely

tanhá

تَنها

á: as (a) in a̲rm

disgusted

motenaffer

مُتِنَفِّر

sick

maríz

مَريض
(bímár)

í: as (ee) in m<u>ee</u>t
á: as (a) in <u>a</u>rm

worried

negarán

نِگَّران

á: as (a) in arm

Quick reference: Feelings

English	Finglisi™	Persian
happy	khoshhál	خوشحال
sad	ghamgín	غَمگین
upset	náráhat	ناراحَت
angry	khashmgín	خَشمگین
frustrated	hers khordan	حِرص خوردَن
hopeless	náomíd	ناأُمید
curious	konjkáv	کُنجکاو
tired	khasteh	خَستِه
fearful/scared	tarsnák	تَرسناک
surprised	mote'ajjeb	مُتعَجِّب
confused	sardargom	سَردَرگُم
bored	hoseleh sar rafteh	حوصِلِه سَر رَفتِه
calm	árám	آرام
excited	hayeján zadeh	هَیِجان زَدِه

Quick reference: Feelings

English	Finglisi™	Persian
Empathetic	delsúzí	دلسوزی
anxious	delvápas	دِلواپَس
proud	eftekhár	اِفتِخار
very good	kheylí khúb	خِیلی خوب
jealous	hasúd	حَسود
satisified	rází	راضی
embarrassed	sharmandeh	شَرمَنده
nervous	a'sabí	عَصَبی
irritated	a'sáb kharáb	أعصاب خَراب
grumpy	bad akhlágh	بَد اخلاق
lonely	tanhá	تَنها
disgusted	motenafer	مُتِنَفِر
sick	maríz	مَریض
worried	negarán	نِگران

www.ingramcontent.com/pod-product-compliance
Lightning Source LLC
Chambersburg PA
CBHW040245100426
42811CB00011B/1154